NFL TODAY

THE STORY OF THE
WASHINGTON REDSKINS

NFL TODAY

THE STORY OF THE WASHINGTON REDSKINS

MICHAEL E. GOODMAN

CREATIVE EDUCATION

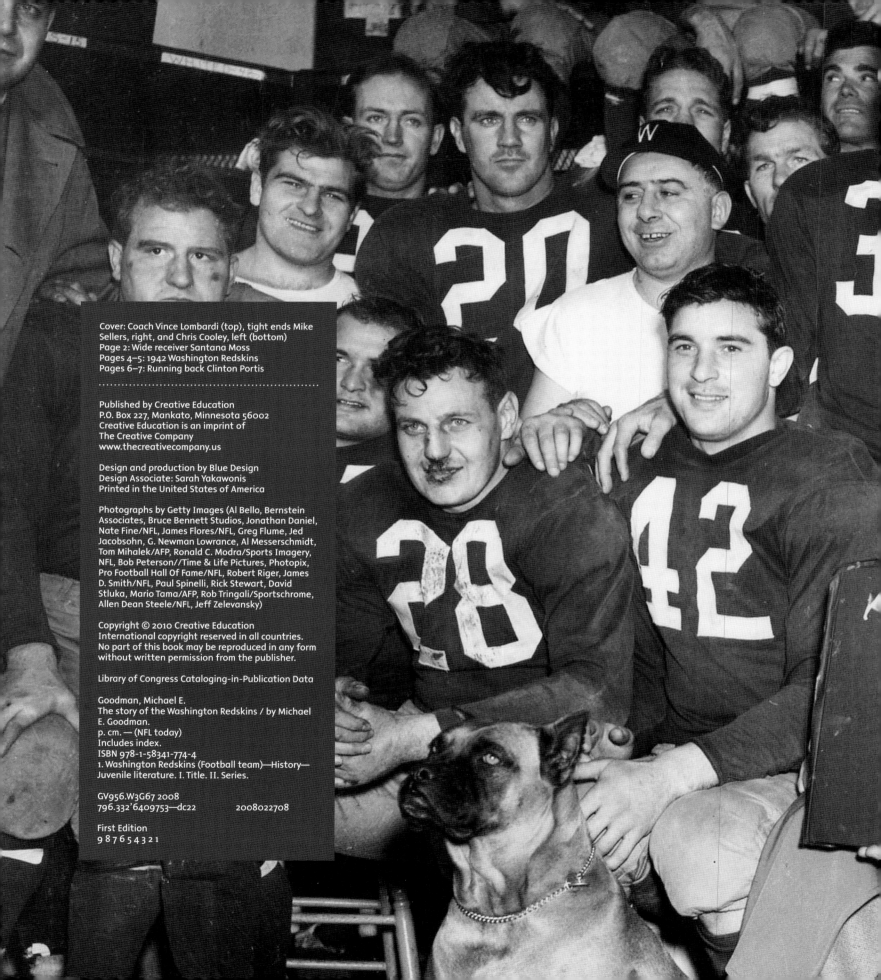

Cover: Coach Vince Lombardi (top), tight ends Mike
Sellers, right, and Chris Cooley, left (bottom)
Page 2: Wide receiver Santana Moss
Pages 4–5: 1942 Washington Redskins
Pages 6–7: Running back Clinton Portis

Published by Creative Education
P.O. Box 227, Mankato, Minnesota 56002
Creative Education is an imprint of
The Creative Company
www.thecreativecompany.us

Design and production by Blue Design
Design Associate: Sarah Yakawonis
Printed in the United States of America

Photographs by Getty Images (Al Bello, Bernstein
Associates, Bruce Bennett Studios, Jonathan Daniel,
Nate Fine/NFL, James Flores/NFL, Greg Flume, Jed
Jacobsohn, G. Newman Lowrance, Al Messerschmidt,
Tom Mihalek/AFP, Ronald C. Modra/Sports Imagery,
NFL, Bob Peterson//Time & Life Pictures, Photopix,
Pro Football Hall Of Fame/NFL, Robert Riger, James
D. Smith/NFL, Paul Spinelli, Rick Stewart, David
Stluka, Mario Tama/AFP, Rob Tringali/Sportschrome,
Allen Dean Steele/NFL, Jeff Zelevansky)

Library of Congress Cataloging-in-Publication Data

Goodman, Michael E.
The story of the Washington Redskins / by Michael
E. Goodman.
p. cm. — (NFL today)
Includes index.
ISBN 978-1-58341-774-4
1. Washington Redskins (Football team)—History—
Juvenile literature. I. Title. II. Series.

GV956.W3G67 2008
796.332'6409753—dc22   2008022708

First Edition
9 8 7 6 5 4 3 2 1

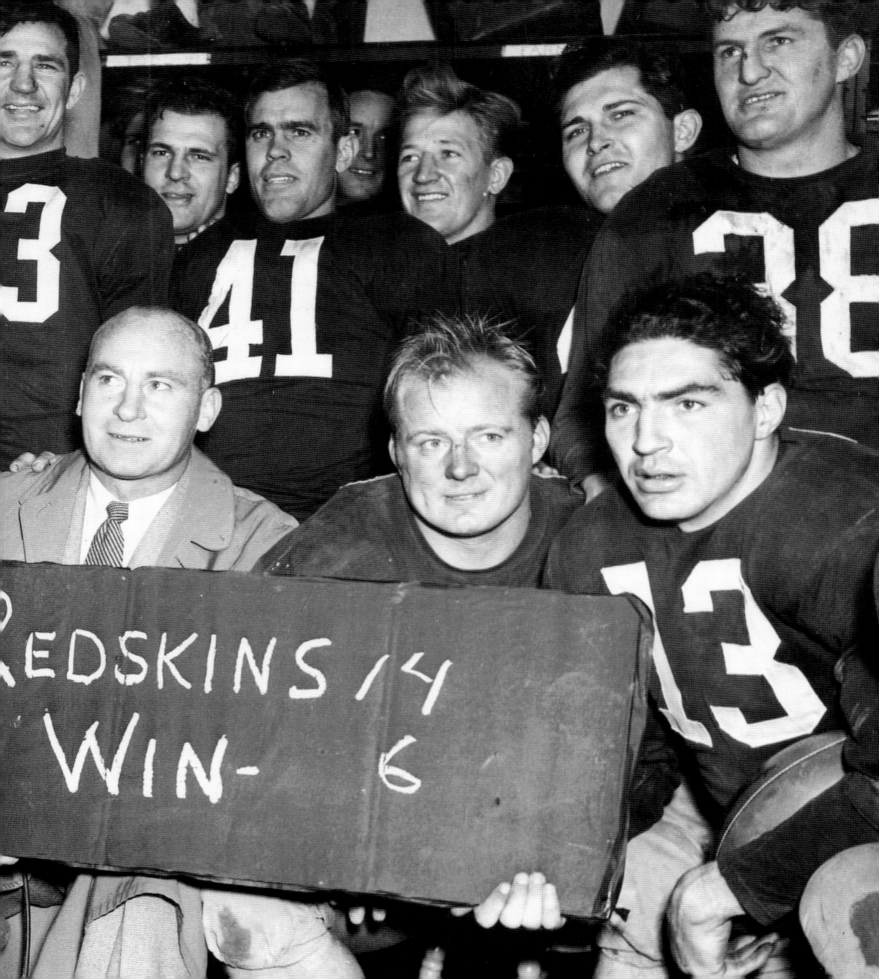

CONTENTS

ON THE SIDELINES

MEET THE REDSKINS

BAUGH IS A DRAW

x - - - - -

X Washington, D.C., has many famous features, including the towering Washington Monument, the elegant United States Capitol, and a decorated football team called the Redskins.

No place in America reflects the country's history better than Washington, D.C. The city is named after the nation's first president, contains monuments to many of its greatest leaders, and proudly displays its most significant documents, such as the Declaration of Independence and the Constitution. Millions of tourists come to Washington each year to see and reflect on the capital's historic places and objects.

In 1937, another group arrived in Washington and began making its own history—the Washington Redskins of the National Football League (NFL). The team had spent its first five seasons in Boston, Massachusetts, before moving to Washington, but it had struggled on the field and at the ticket office. So franchise owner George Preston Marshall, who owned other businesses in Washington, decided to give his club a fresh start by moving it to the nation's capital.

The 1937 Redskins adopted more than just a new hometown. They also embraced a new look that Marshall

Sammy Baugh sharpened his revolutionary passing skills in high school by throwing balls through a car tire suspended in a tree. **X**

hoped would draw more fan attention than the team had received in Boston. The Redskins were decked out in new uniforms of gold and burgundy and, more importantly, featured a new star: rookie quarterback Sammy Baugh.

Baugh had earned the nickname "Slingin' Sammy" at Texas Christian University because of his skill as a passer. In the 1930s, passing played a much lesser role in football than it does today. However, once Baugh began slinging passes around the field, football was changed forever. As *New York Times* sportswriter Arthur Daley noted, "It was Baugh who revolutionized football and altered all previous offensive strategies."

With Baugh, offensive end Wayne Millner, and halfback Cliff Battles leading the way, the Redskins topped the NFL's

GEORGE PRESTON MARSHALL

TEAM FOUNDER, OWNER
REDSKINS SEASONS: 1932-62

From the time he founded the Redskins until he retired due to poor health, George Preston Marshall (pictured, left) controlled every aspect of the franchise. Known as "The Big Chief," Marshall had an opinion on everything that had to do with the Redskins. He would fire coaches in a flash and often send suggestions for plays to his coach during a game. He would even telephone instructions from his private box to the team's band director about what songs to play. The one thing Marshall would not do for many years was sign an African American player for the Redskins. He was finally forced to change his mind in 1962 when the federal government threatened to kick the team out of RFK Stadium if it didn't hire black players. Marshall was a true pioneer of professional football and created many of the rules that helped the sport grow, including those that permitted more passing and created hash marks for marking the placement of the football on the field. He may have been strong-minded, but his primary aim was always to improve the Redskins.

ON THE SIDELINES

HAIL TO THE REDSKINS

George Preston Marshall was a showman who believed that fans attending a Redskins contest should be entertained before, during, and after a game. So in 1937, the team's first year in Washington, he put together an all-volunteer band to play the fans into and out of the stadium and to put on halftime "extravaganzas." The Washington Redskins Marching Band that Marshall organized was the first of its kind, and its 150 members are still performing at FedExField today. It has also put on special performances for team victory parades, starting with the one honoring the team's first NFL championship in 1937. One year after forming the band, Marshall decided that the club needed its own fight song. Famed dance-band leader Barnee Breeskin, a close friend of Marshall's, wrote a spirited melody to go with lyrics written by Marshall's wife Corinne Griffith, a star of 1920s silent films. The song, "Hail to the Redskins," is still first in the hearts of Washington football fans, who loudly proclaim at each game, "Hail to the Redskins! Hail to victory! Braves on the warpath, fight for old D.C."

Eastern Division in their first season in Washington. Then they traveled to Chicago to take on the powerful Bears in the NFL Championship Game. Washington's chances looked slim when Baugh, battered by Bears defenders, could barely drag himself into the locker room at halftime. But in the second half, a taped-up Baugh completed two long touchdown passes to Millner to lead the Redskins to a 28–21 win and the team's first NFL title.

Baugh played three major roles for the Redskins during his amazing career. In addition to being the starting quarterback, he was also the team's best defensive back and an outstanding punter. He excelled in all three roles as he led Washington to a second NFL East title in 1940 and another championship game against Chicago. This time, though, the Bears got their revenge by walloping the Redskins 73–0 in the most lopsided championship game of all time.

The Redskins quickly rebounded after their humiliating loss. Behind Baugh and running backs Frank Filchock and Andy Farkas, they topped the NFL East in 1942, 1943, and 1945 and earned a second league title by defeating the Bears in the 1942 championship game.

With Baugh leading the way, the Redskins drew large crowds to Griffith Stadium in Washington. And, because the team was based farther south than any other franchise in the NFL, it became the "home team" for millions of football fans in Southern states. The team's popularity also encouraged George Preston Marshall to set up the NFL's first radio network in 1944 to broadcast games and to make league history again in 1950 by broadcasting 'Skins games on that relatively new invention, the television.

By the time Slingin' Sammy retired in 1952, he had set almost all of the NFL's passing records and even established season and career punting records that still stand today. His number 33 jersey is the only one that has ever been officially retired by the Redskins.

Following Baugh's retirement, the Redskins entered a dark period in their history. The team managed to achieve only three winning records throughout the 1950s and '60s. Still, Washington fans loudly cheered the efforts of such standouts as undersized quarterback Eddie LeBaron. The "Little General" stood 5-foot-9 and weighed only 168 pounds, but he thrilled fans with his scrambling maneuvers and ability to pass around and over much bigger defenders. Other fan favorites included two-way stars Gene Brito, who played both offensive and defensive end, and Dick James, the team's top rusher and defensive back.

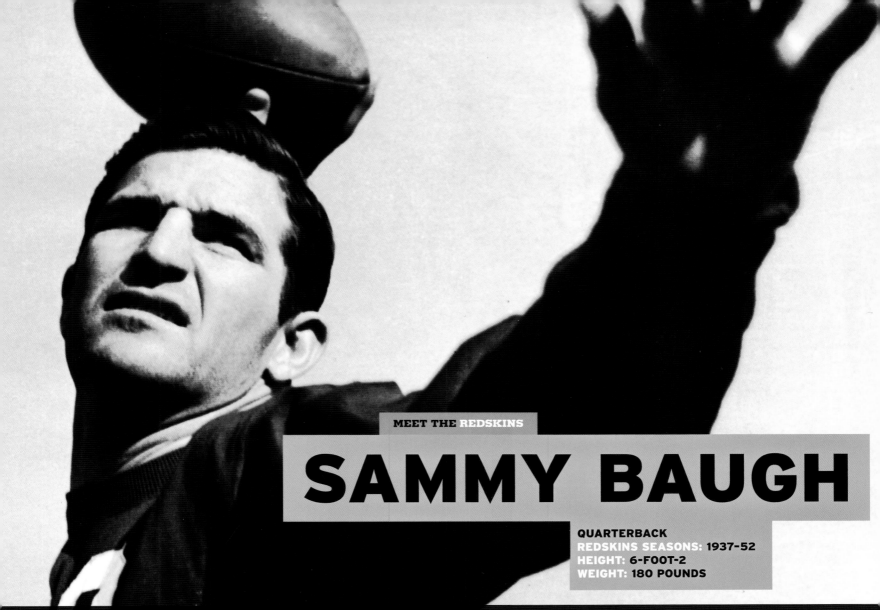

SAMMY BAUGH

QUARTERBACK
REDSKINS SEASONS: 1937-52
HEIGHT: 6-FOOT-2
WEIGHT: 180 POUNDS

"Slingin' Sammy" Baugh was one of pro football's first great passers. Born in Texas farming country, Baugh first made headlines as a football and baseball star at Texas Christian University. Redskins owner George Preston Marshall decided Baugh was the ideal player to win over fans in Washington, where the team would be moving in 1937. To convince Baugh to sign with the Redskins instead of baseball's St. Louis Cardinals, Marshall raised his salary offer to a lofty $8,000. The big contract turned out to be a bargain. At Baugh's first training camp, his new coach, Ray Flaherty, put him through some tough passing drills. Flaherty marked a spot on the field and said, "When the receiver reaches this spot, I want you to hit him in the eye with the ball." Baugh quickly responded, "Which eye?" For the next 15 years, Baugh impressed coaches and fans with his passing accuracy and his toughness. He led the NFL in passing six times and, in 1963, was in the first class of players inducted into the Pro Football Hall of Fame.

[15]

SONNY AND SAM STEP UP

X Sam Huff
(number 70) was one
of football's biggest
defensive stars in
the early 1960s, a
linebacker renowned
for his rare blend of
strength, speed, agility,
and instinct.

The Redskins' fortunes began to improve in the mid-1960s, thanks to several strategic moves. In 1962, Washington acquired running back Bobby Mitchell from the Cleveland Browns. Mitchell was the first African American player in the team's history, and he paved the way for other black stars in Washington. An outstanding runner, pass receiver, and kick returner, Mitchell led the NFL in pass receiving his first two seasons in Washington. The Redskins were the last NFL team to sign black players, largely because of the prejudices of their owner, and this sad fact may have been one reason that other teams outperformed the 'Skins during these years.

Washington's management made two other key moves in 1964, trading with the Philadelphia Eagles for quarterback Sonny Jurgensen and with the New York Giants for linebacker Sam Huff. Jurgensen—known for his strong arm, slow feet, and tremendous confidence—revived memories of Sammy Baugh in Washington fans. He teamed with Mitchell and rookie wide receiver Charley Taylor to turn the sluggish Redskins offense into a highflying aerial attack. "Back then, the NFL had other great quarterbacks like John Unitas and Bart Starr, but Sonny was the guy," said Taylor. "He had a feel for the game—he made it easy for his receivers."

X Sonny Jurgensen became a kind of folk hero in Washington, a fearless leader who always seemed to unload the ball just before getting hit.

Huff, who had helped lead the Giants to six NFL championship games before coming to Washington, brought an intensity to the Redskins' defense that had been missing. His philosophy of the game was very simple: "Get the man with the football!" he would shout at his teammates. Sonny and Sam quickly bonded together as team leaders and as close friends. They remained with the Redskins even after they retired as players, becoming part of the club's radio broadcasting team for more than 35 years.

Even with the additions of Jurgensen and Huff, the Redskins didn't become winners until 1969, when Hall of Fame coach Vince Lombardi came out of retirement to re-energize the team. Before the 1969 season opener, Lombardi reminded his new players that he had never coached a losing club. "And nothing is going to change that," he insisted.

X Vince Lombardi's arrival in 1969 sparked dreams of championships in America's capital, but the legendary coach passed away only a year later.

ON THE SIDELINES

LOMBARDI'S LEGACY

Vince Lombardi is best known for building the Green Bay Packers into one of the NFL's most impressive dynasties in the 1960s. But the year he spent in Washington—1969—may have been the greatest tribute to his legacy as a winner. In that one season, he helped transform the Redskins from a bumbling, sub-.500 franchise that hadn't posted a winning season in 13 years into an NFL powerhouse for the next 2 decades. Lombardi made several key on-field changes. First, he opened up the team's offense, helping quarterback Sonny Jurgensen and receiver Charley Taylor become the most fearsome tandem in the league. Then he made rookie Larry Brown (pictured), an unheralded eighth-round draft pick, his primary running back. Brown would lead the Redskins in rushing for six straight seasons. Even more important were the changes Lombardi made inside his players. "Lombardi was able to get inside your heart and mind and lead you to levels way above your abilities and skills," said guard Vince Promuto. Suddenly, there was a winning atmosphere in Washington's RFK Stadium that would last long after Lombardi's untimely death.

Inspired by their coach's confidence, the Redskins finally broke their losing streak, finishing with a 7–5–2 record in 1969. Spirits were high in Washington, but they soon fell again. During the off-season, Coach Lombardi died suddenly from cancer. The Redskins reverted to their losing ways in 1970, but they were ready for a major turnaround when George Allen took over the reins the following year.

Allen, a big winner as coach of the Los Angeles Rams, didn't want to take the time to develop young talent in Washington. Instead, he immediately began trading away future draft choices for established stars. Among the veterans who arrived in Washington were quarterback Billy Kilmer, linebacker Jack Pardee, and safety Richie Petitbon, all of whom were in their 30s. Fans and writers soon began calling the Redskins the "Over the Hill Gang."

Allen's gamble paid off. The Over the Hill Gang made the playoffs in 1971 after posting a 9–4–1 record. It was the club's first postseason appearance in 25 years. The next year, the Redskins captured the National Football Conference (NFC) championship and earned the club's first Super Bowl berth, only to fall to the undefeated Miami Dolphins in the championship game, 14–7.

SUPER SEASONS
IN WASHINGTON

Coach Allen's Redskins made the playoffs three more times between 1973 and 1977 but failed to reach the Super Bowl again. In 1978, Allen was replaced by former Redskins linebacker Jack Pardee, who promoted backup quarterback Joe Theismann to the starting role. "You've paid your dues," Pardee told his new passer. "Now it's time to take charge and get this team rolling again. The future is now."

While Jurgensen and Kilmer had been strictly drop-back passers, Theismann loved to scramble to keep opposing defensive linemen off-balance. Joining Theismann in the backfield was running back John Riggins, whom teammates called "The Diesel" because he roared through the line like a powerful truck. In 1980, the Redskins added another offensive star by drafting young receiver Art Monk out of Syracuse University.

Despite their offensive improvements, the Redskins remained a middle-of-the-pack team until Joe Gibbs took over as coach in 1981. Gibbs rebuilt the team's defense around nose guard Dave Butz and ends Dexter Manley and Charles Mann. To the offensive line he added several huge blockers,

John Riggins was a colorful character known for his wild hairstyles and often outlandish quotes, but there was nothing flashy about his bulldozing, straight-ahead rushing style. **X**

JOHN RIGGINS

RUNNING BACK
REDSKINS SEASONS: 1976-79, 1981-85
HEIGHT: 6-FOOT-2
WEIGHT: 230 POUNDS

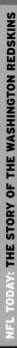

Ask Redskins fans to name the most famous play in franchise history, and they'll likely reply, "John Riggins's game-winning, 43-yard touchdown run in Super Bowl XVII." That touchdown jaunt was just one of many outstanding runs that Riggins made during his career in Washington. He still holds team career records for most rushing attempts, rushing yards, and rushing touchdowns. Riggins had an unusual combination of power, speed, and cockiness. He was also a little crazy. He once came into training camp sporting a Mohawk haircut. Another year, he showed up wearing only shorts and a derby hat with a feather in it. Riggins started his pro career with the New York Jets and then signed with the Redskins in 1976. He left the team before the 1980 season over a contract dispute but returned one year later after a meeting with new coach Joe Gibbs. "I'm bored, I'm broke, and I'm back," he announced to fans before resuming his record-breaking career. In 1992, Riggins was inducted into the Pro Football Hall of Fame.

known affectionately as "The Hogs." Gibbs's Redskins quickly rose to the top of the NFC and reached the Super Bowl in the coach's second season at the helm.

In January 1983, exactly 10 years after their first Super Bowl appearance, the Redskins faced off against the Miami Dolphins once again for the NFL championship. This time the result would be different. Theismann played brilliantly, tossing two touchdown passes. But his most important move was handing the ball off to Riggins on a fourth-down play early in the fourth quarter. Miami was ahead 17–13, and everyone was expecting Riggins to simply dive forward a yard for the first down. Instead, The Diesel slid toward his left, broke through the tightly packed defenders, and raced 43 yards for a touchdown that sealed the Redskins' first Super Bowl triumph.

Washington was even more dominant the next year, breaking several league scoring records en route to a 14–2 season. The team reached the Super Bowl once again but fell to the Los Angeles Raiders, 38–9, failing to win a second consecutive title. Still, many Redskins players and fans believed that the 1983 club was the franchise's best ever. "We were the best team in the history of Washington football," said Theismann, who was named the league's Most Valuable

NFL TODAY: THE STORY OF THE WASHINGTON REDSKINS

HOGGING THE GLORY

When most fans think about the 1983 Super Bowl, they recall John Riggins's game-breaking touchdown run. What they don't always remember is who opened up the huge hole in the Miami Dolphins' defense through which Riggins ran. Those players were 300-pound tackle Joe Jacoby and 275-pound guard Russ Grimm, and they were charter members of one of the most famous offensive lines of all time—"The Hogs." The Hogs got their nickname from the team's offensive coordinator, Joe Bugel. "A Hog," Bugel explained, "is a guy who gets down and does a dirty job without wanting to be beautiful." In the 1980s, the tackles, guards, centers, and tight ends who made up The Hogs became almost as well known in Washington as the team's backs and receivers. Many Redskins fans showed up at RFK Stadium each week wearing hog noses, hog hats, or hog T-shirts to show their love for their hard-working heroes. The Hogs also included one player who didn't toil on the offensive line—Riggins. He was admitted because "he has the personality of a Hog," said veteran tight end George Starke.

Player (MVP) in 1983. "But that will never be known because we didn't win a Super Bowl."

By 1987, a new lineup was in place in Washington. Theismann and Riggins had both retired and been replaced by quarterback Doug Williams and running back George Rogers. The Redskins dominated the NFC East Division with an 11–4 record during the regular season. In the postseason, Williams led Washington to victories over the Chicago Bears and Minnesota Vikings and into another Super Bowl.

Facing the Denver Broncos in the Super Bowl, the Redskins quickly fell behind 10–0. Then Williams let his strong right arm take over, tossing a Super Bowl-record four second-quarter touchdown passes to spark an amazing turnaround. The Redskins went on to win 42–10, and Williams was named the game's MVP. After the game, Williams was asked about the remarkable comeback. "It was destined," he said simply. "It was in the cards."

After suffering a back injury the next season, Williams was replaced by big (6-foot-4 and 230 pounds) and tough quarterback Mark Rypien. The young passer led the club to winning seasons in 1989, 1990, and 1991. Then, in the 1991 playoffs, Rypien earned his own Super Bowl MVP award when he guided the Redskins to a decisive 37–24 championship victory over the Buffalo Bills.

X Doug Williams made football history in 1987 by becoming the first African American quarterback to lead his team to a Super Bowl, earning a ring in Super Bowl XXII.

X ------------------------------

Coach Gibbs spent one more season directing the Redskins before retiring in 1993. He left as the most successful coach in franchise history. In 12 seasons, Gibbs's teams had reached the playoffs 8 times and appeared in 4 Super Bowls, winning 3 of them.

Gibbs's departure was followed by a decline in the team's fortunes. The Redskins dropped to the middle of the NFC East standings under coaches Richie Petitbon and Norv Turner and didn't reach the playoffs again until 1999, despite the heroics of such players as running back Terry Allen, kick returner Brian Mitchell, and cornerback Darrell Green.

Before the 1999 season, the Redskins made a key addition, drafting cornerback Champ Bailey out of the University of Georgia. With a defense featuring Bailey and an offense led by quarterback Brad Johnson and running back Stephen Davis, the Redskins went 10–6 in 1999. They thrilled the fans who packed FedExField (the team's home since 1997) with several stirring comebacks and came within one point of reaching the NFC Championship Game that year. "We didn't have a lot of big names on the team," recalled linebacker Eddie Mason. "We had a bunch of guys who played well together and were tight like a family. We

X After being deployed mainly as a blocking fullback for three years, Stephen Davis stepped into the spotlight as the Redskins' featured back in 1999, galloping for an NFC-best 1,405 yards.

ART MONK

WIDE RECEIVER
REDSKINS SEASONS: 1980-93
HEIGHT: 6-FOOT-3
WEIGHT: 210 POUNDS

On October 13, 1992, Art Monk caught his 820th pass to become the NFL's all-time leader in pass receptions. (Monk's record has since been broken by five other players.) That record-breaking pass was a tribute both to Monk's skill as a receiver and his remarkable consistency. From his rookie season in 1980 until he left Washington in 1993, Monk caught 50 or more passes 9 times and topped the 100 mark in 1984. "Art was quiet about his work but very loud with his results," said Washington quarterback Mark Rypien. Added Redskins general manager Charley Casserly, "There was never a classier player in the franchise's history, or in league history, than Art Monk. You always knew the team would be getting Art Monk's best effort day in and day out." Monk was the team's top draft choice out of New York's Syracuse University in 1980 and quickly became a star, winning the award as the NFL's top offensive rookie that year. Monk was a dominant receiver throughout the 1980s and was voted to the Pro Bowl three times during the decade.

knew how to win and come together. That is what it takes....
It was a tremendous feeling."

Unfortunately, the excitement generated by the 1999
team soon faded in the new millennium, and the club's new
owner, 35-year-old billionaire Daniel Snyder, quickly became
impatient. Using the same daring tactics that helped him
achieve success in business, Snyder made a number of
expensive but misguided decisions. He spent millions of
dollars bringing in veteran stars such as defensive end Bruce
Smith, cornerback Deion Sanders, and quarterback Jeff
George to recharge the team. But such additions seemed to
destroy the chemistry that the 1999 team had possessed.

X Nicknamed
"Prime Time," Deion
Sanders was past his
prime when he arrived
in Washington in 2000
but still managed to
snag four interceptions.

Snyder also made rash decisions about coaches. After the 'Skins slumped at the end of the 2000 season, Snyder fired Norv Turner and replaced him with veteran coach Marty Schottenheimer. When Schottenheimer's club went a mere 8–8 in his first year, Snyder decided to bring in college "supercoach" Steve Spurrier to take over the Redskins.

Spurrier, a former NFL quarterback who had won the 1996 college national championship as coach of the Florida Gators, was thrilled with the challenge and predicted a bright future for the Redskins. "To coach in this city, with the biggest stadium in the NFL, with the best fans—we're going to turn FedExField into the loudest stadium in the country," he said.

Unfortunately, much of the noise that Spurrier heard in the Redskins' stadium over the next two years consisted of boos. Despite the additions of strong-armed quarterback Patrick Ramsey and wide receiver Laveranues Coles to enhance the offense and the presence of All-Pro defenders such as Bailey and linebacker LaVar Arrington, Spurrier's teams suffered through losing seasons in both 2003 and 2004 before the coach resigned and returned to the college ranks.

Faced with making a fourth coaching change in only five years, Snyder decided that only one man possessed the right combination of football savvy, coaching style, and a history

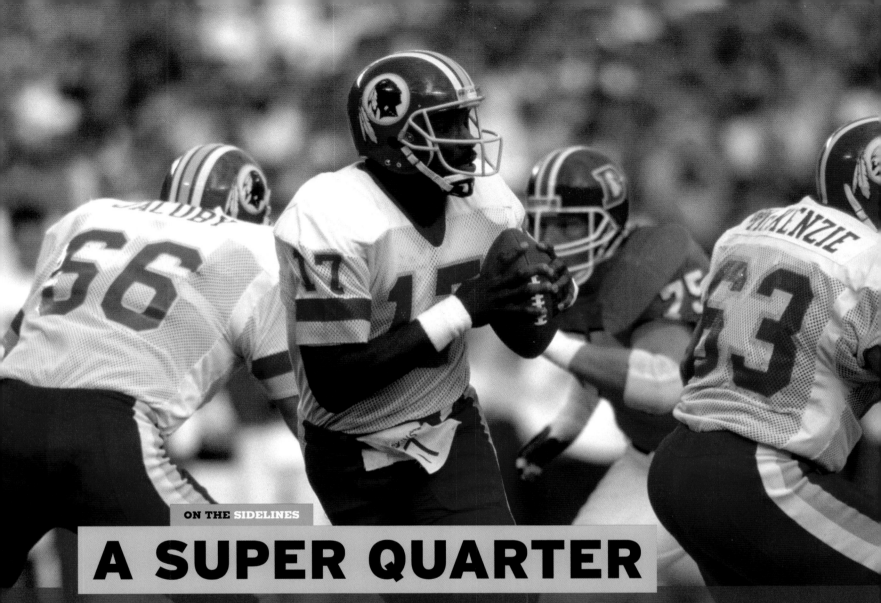

A SUPER QUARTER

Doug Williams had a brief career as a Redskins quarterback, but the one nearly perfect quarter he played during Super Bowl XXII on January 31, 1988, earned him an honored place in the team's history forever. "We scored 35 points in 18 plays—that's execution at its very best," recalled Williams. "Offensively, we were in a zone. It didn't matter who we were playing; they weren't going to stop us." The five-touchdown outburst by the Redskins in the second quarter of the game turned a 10–0 Denver Broncos lead into a 35–10 Washington rout. From there, the 'Skins coasted to a 42–10 victory. Amazingly, Williams nearly missed out on his historic quarter. Near the end of the first period, he hyperextended his left knee and limped off the field. He was back for the Redskins' next offensive series, however, and the fireworks began. Starting with a Super Bowl-record 80-yard touchdown pass to wide receiver Ricky Sanders, Williams completed 18 of 29 passes during the quarter for 340 yards and 4 touchdowns. "Doug was the right man in the right place," said coach Joe Gibbs.

JOE GIBBS

COACH
REDSKINS SEASONS:
1981-92, 2004-07

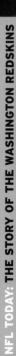

During the 1970s, the Redskins were a solid but predictable team. That began to change when Joe Gibbs was hired as coach in 1981. Gibbs had built a reputation for being an offensive genius as an assistant coach with the San Diego Chargers. Upon arriving in Washington, he immediately began shaking things up. Gibbs drafted several outstanding young offensive linemen to block for his quarterback, convinced running back John Riggins to abandon retirement and return to the team, and began transforming the Redskins from a "grind-it-out" club into one that continually surprised opposing defenders by slashing through or passing over them. "Gibbs is a man of perception and a coach of deception," said one Washington sportswriter. In his second year in Washington, Gibbs led the Redskins to their first Super Bowl triumph. The 'Skins would play in three more Super Bowls and win two more championships before Gibbs retired in 1992 to focus on his other main interest— directing a successful team of race-car drivers. Gibbs came out of retirement in 2004 and led the Redskins back to the playoffs one year later.

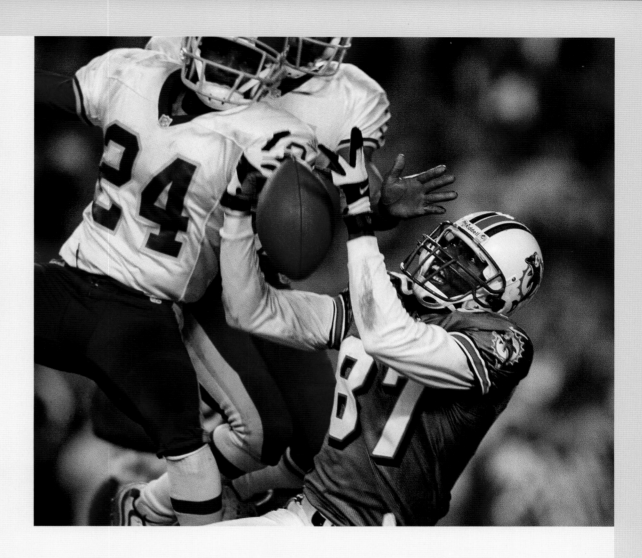

of success needed to return the Redskins to their former glory—Joe Gibbs. So, on January 9, 2004, he surprised the sports world by announcing that Gibbs would be coming back to Washington after an 11-year absence. Appearing at a press conference that day, Gibbs told reporters that he purposely was not wearing any of the Super Bowl rings that he had earned in his earlier stint with the Redskins. "We're focused on the future," he said. "I love the challenge of doing something that's almost undoable."

X Champ Bailey (pictured) reminded many fans of Darrell Green, as both were smart cornerbacks with enough speed to blanket any receiver.

SUCCESS AND SADNESS

X

A safety the size of a linebacker, Sean Taylor became known to his teammates as "Meast" (half-man, half-beast) on account of the vicious hits he laid on opponents.

Facing his new challenge head-on, Gibbs began making significant changes. He engineered a trade of All-Pro players with the Broncos, sending Champ Bailey to Denver in exchange for running back Clinton Portis, whose straight-ahead running style reminded older Washington fans of John Riggins. He also signed free-agent quarterback Mark Brunell to direct the offense and traded for wide receiver Santana Moss, whose blazing speed could help open up the Redskins' passing attack.

Gibbs knew he had made the right decisions, but it would take time to re-establish good team chemistry. The 'Skins averaged fewer than 20 points per game in 2004 and finished with a dismal 6–10 record. They got off to a rocky start in 2005 as well, and fans worried that the team might suffer two straight losing seasons for the first time ever under Gibbs. Then the Redskins rebounded, winning their last five games and roaring into the playoffs with a 10–6 record.

They continued their winning ways in the postseason against the Tampa Bay Buccaneers. Led by defensive standouts such as linebacker Marcus Washington and safety Sean Taylor, the Redskins hounded Tampa Bay quarterback Chris Simms all afternoon on their way to a 17–10 win. The defense remained strong in the team's next playoff game

against the Seattle Seahawks, but the offense sputtered. The result was a 20–10, season-ending loss. "We hit a rough point this year when we were 5–6, and guys could have pointed fingers," said Portis. "But nobody did. We won a tough one last week and lost a tough one this week. We've got more to look forward to next year."

However, 2006 turned out to be a year of transition for the Redskins. Portis was injured for much of the season, and Brunell proved to be ineffective. By November, Gibbs decided to replace his veteran signal-caller with second-year quarterback Jason Campbell, who had been an All-American at Auburn University in Alabama. The end result was a 5–11 season that most Redskins fans wanted to forget.

But few fans would ever forget what happened the next year. Led by a rapidly maturing Campbell, along with a recovered Portis, Moss, and tight end Chris Cooley, the 'Skins won five of their first eight games and seemed to be headed for the playoffs by midseason. Then they lost three tight contests in a row and appeared to be in a free fall.

Things turned from terrible to tragic in early December 2007, when All-Pro safety Taylor was shot to death by burglars in his Miami home. Gibbs gathered his players together and tried to console them. "Sometimes in life, maybe some of

ONE MORE COMEBACK?

In 1999, the Redskins were the "comeback kids." Led by quarterback Brad Johnson (pictured), they staged several exciting come-from-behind victories, winning two contests in overtime and another on a last-second field goal. So there was no panic on the Washington sideline with less than two minutes remaining in the team's second-round playoff game with the Tampa Bay Buccaneers—even though the Redskins were trailing 14–13. Washington's defense made a key stop and forced a Tampa Bay punt. Then Johnson took over. He completed three passes for 22 yards, and running back Larry Centers rushed for 7 more as the Redskins drove from their 38 to the Tampa Bay 33-yard line. With time running out, Washington set up for a game-winning, 51-yard field goal. But it never happened. Center Dan Turk's hike to Johnson, who was set to hold the ball, was low and off-line. Johnson scooped up the ball, rose, and attempted to get off a pass that fell incomplete. Needing one more comeback on their way to another Super Bowl, the Redskins came up one point short.

ON THE SIDELINES

THE RIVALRY

When the Redskins defeated the Dallas Cowboys in the final game of the 2007 season to complete their remarkable turnaround to reach the playoffs, it marked another highlight in perhaps the greatest rivalry in professional football. The Redskins and Cowboys have been playing hard-fought games ever since Dallas entered the NFL in 1960. In fact, Washington's only win in 1960 came against the expansion Cowboys. Since the two teams have always been in the same NFC division, they have played each other at least twice a year—nearly 100 times in all. The Cowboys hold the edge in total victories in the series, but the Redskins have won two of the most important games, topping Dallas in the NFC Championship Game in both 1972 and 1982 on their way to their first two Super Bowls. Other key Washington victories included late-season, playoff-clinching wins in 1976 and 1984. "It's the Redskins versus the Cowboys; it doesn't get much better than that," said famed television commentator John Madden before a recent battle between the rivals. "It just sounds like football."

the best things happen to you after you have been kind of crushed," he said. He hoped the team would come together over the next few weeks both to grieve for their teammate and to finish the season in a positive way.

The 'Skins made a heroic comeback, winning their last four contests to earn a Wild Card berth in the postseason. Despite falling to the Seattle Seahawks in the first round of the playoffs, the Redskins remained formidable in 2008. Under new head coach Jim Zorn (who was hired following Gibbs's second retirement), and behind the offensive leadership of Campbell, Washington stayed near the top of the always-

X Known as a prankster off the field, running back Clinton Portis was all business on game days, leading the NFL with 325 carries in 2007.

X Under new coach Jim Zorn, the 2008 Redskins started with a bang, opening the season with a surprising 6–2 mark.

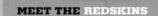

DARRELL GREEN

CORNERBACK
REDSKINS SEASONS: 1983–2002
HEIGHT: 5-FOOT-8
WEIGHT: 185 POUNDS

When Darrell Green first joined the Redskins in 1983, he was known primarily for his speed, as he could run the 40-yard dash in a remarkable 4.13 seconds. His skill as a cornerback soon shown through, too. During a playoff game against the Los Angeles Rams, the rookie intercepted a pass and returned it 72 yards for a touchdown to help seal a Washington victory. Green played 19 more seasons with the Redskins and barely slowed down at all. By the time he retired in 2002, he held club records for most interceptions, most interceptions returned for touchdowns, most games played, and most games started. "He had great, great feet and switched directions so well," said Dallas Cowboys receiver Alvin Harper, who battled Green for many years. "If you faked one way, and he closed that way, and then you went another way, he would whirl around so fast it was like he was on the same path with you the whole time." A seven-time Pro-Bowler, Green was also named NFL Man of the Year in 1996 for his charitable work in the Washington area.

competitive NFC East all season long, finishing 8–8.

For more than 200 years, Washington, D.C., has been at the center of American history. And for more than 70 years, the Washington Redskins have represented the nation's capital on the NFL gridiron. With a proud history that features five world championships and some of the game's greatest legends, the Redskins hope to soon make Washington the football capital of the United States once again.

X Young quarterback Jason Campbell set a team record in 2007 and 2008 by throwing 252 straight passes without an interception.

INDEX